God In My Life

_____

Rita Kay Crowder Roberts

TEACH Services, Inc.
P U B L I S H I N G
www.TEACHServices.com • (800) 367-1844

Copyright © 2018 Rita Kay Crowder Roberts

Copyright © 2018 TEACH Services, Inc.

ISBN-13: 978-1-4796-0972-7 (Paperback)

ISBN-13: 978-1-4796-0972-7 (ePub)

Library of Congress Control Number: 2018950378

TEACH Services, Inc.

P U B L I S H I N G

www.TEACHServices.com • (800) 367-1844

Dedication

I bow humbly before God, my Heavenly Father, thanking Him for being in my life, allowing me to be a part of these wonderful miracles, and to share the story of them with all who will read. I also thank Him for making these many blessings out of the tragedies. Without His hand of grace I would not be alive to write this book. He is so awesome!

"That I may publish with the voice of thanksgiving, and tell of all Thy wondrous works" (Ps. 26:7).

A Word of Thanks ...

To Penney Smith, Susan McCoy Hristov, and My Children—
For all of their time, work, and encouragement.

Table of Contents

Prologue

I've got to tell you to start with that at this writing I'm sixty-plus years old. It's sad to realize that it's taken me that many years to discover that God IS in my life. He's been here the whole time, but I didn't realize it. Miracle after miracle, He's been right here. But of course, if you are reading this you have been a product of His miracles, too. Actually, YOU are a miracle. Anyone who has witnessed the birth of a baby knows that is a miracle in itself.

My friend Bea and I used to walk every morning up into the woods to "our rock." It was big enough for both of us to sit comfortably beside each other on it and talk and pray together. My favorite expression was always "that's awesome," and I have used it many times in conversation at that very special rock.

One day, Bea, who was my elder in age, said to me, "Awesome is the best word we have in the English language, so we need to save that for anything to do with God—for respect and honor for Him alone."

She's right, of course. So I had to practice NOT using it for other things, and save it for God only. Therefore, in my writings, I use *awesome* only for God.

The Crib

Even before I was born, God's hand was already orchestrating my life.

After Mother discovered she was pregnant with me, she excitedly began making plans for her new baby. Since she and Daddy lived in the country in a big house, affectionately called the "Orchard House," they would have to drive twenty miles to the city to buy a baby crib. There were no official "baby stores" back then and options were limited. Having never looked for baby things before they had no idea where to go to get a baby crib. Because of this they had a very hard time deciding where to buy it. Where would be the best deal? Back in the 1940's, you just couldn't quickly call all the stores and ask, and nobody had even heard of the internet and online shopping—that wouldn't be a thing for another five decades.

Finally one night it was decided that they would "crib shop" the next day. Mother prayed, "Lord, please show me where to go buy the best crib for our new baby."

The next morning was sunny and beautiful. Mother started fixing breakfast and was still asking God where to go when, right outside the open kitchen window, just inches from her, a little bird landed on a bush and chirped "Ster-Chi, Ster-Chi, Ster-Chi," and then flew away.

"Oh, yes, Sterchi's," Mother thought immediately, and told Daddy about the bird and its message. So they drove over to Sterchi's Department Store and, sure enough, there they found a very good deal on a beautiful baby crib! God had used a little bird to tell them where to go to find the crib He had chosen for me!

"Delight thyself also in the Lord; and He shall give thee the desires of thine heart" (Ps. 37:4).

The Dump Truck

When I was a baby, Mother and Daddy and I lived in a small, one-bedroom house on the side of a busy road. The house was located beside a sharp curve in the road and from its large picture window in the living room one could look out across the porch and yard toward that part of the road. My baby crib sat right in front of that picture window. On this particular evening, Mother had fed me, rocked me, and sang me to sleep with her sweet songs. Just as she was laying me down in my crib I started crying. She picked me up and held me to rock and sing some more. Back to sleep I went.

Then, as she lay me gently in my crib a second time, I started crying again; only this time it was more of a scream! Baffled, Mother picked me up. This was so strange! Usually I went right to sleep. But, since my mother never let me just cry, she held me close and walked around the room singing. Mother always believed that if a baby has the right kind of attention and still cries, that cry means something and she was determined to figure it out so I would not need to cry. Crying means SOMETHING.

No matter what she did, my crying kept getting worse. Not only did I start crying every time Mother just started walking toward the crib, but I started screaming louder as she even walked around in the small living room. In desperation, Mother carried me into her bedroom just off of the living room. As soon as she crossed the threshold into her bedroom I stopped screaming and went sound asleep! Thinking it was ok to put me back in the crib, she started back toward it and I once again started screaming. Like before, when she crossed into her room, I went to sleep. Mother, finally giving up on the idea of the crib that day, laid me in the middle of her bed and I slept away. She walked around her bed to the foot, where the ironing board was, to finish the ironing before Daddy came home for supper.

> *No matter what she did, my crying kept getting worse.*

Just as she picked up the iron, a huge dump truck loaded with rocks and driving too fast missed the sharp curve on the highway out front and plowed across the yard into the front porch, crashing through the picture window, and totally demolishing my baby crib.

Before I even knew Him, the God in my life saved me and my mother by getting us both out of that room just in time!

"For He shall give His angels charge over thee, to keep thee in all thy ways" (Ps. 91:11).

The Fall

"Mrs. Crowder, I have to leave a few minutes early, today," the babysitter told my mother. "I will leave Rita Kay out on the front lawn of the hospital where you can watch her through the window until you get off work. She can play with her new big ball."

Mother only had a few more minutes until she got off work from her nursing job at the hospital. The front lawn of the hospital was very grassy and away from motor traffic. I was a toddler, just beginning to perfect walking, and was delighted with my big, new ball which (I was told later) was barely small enough for me to hold with my tiny arms. Mother checked the window as she was getting off work when she saw me carrying my big ball up the ramp to the other part of the hospital. She rushed out the front door of the hospital to try to stop me. As she was reaching the ramp, she watched in horror as the ball slipped out of my hands and went over the edge of the ramp, eight feet down to the cement walk below, with me diving over after it, falling all the way down and landing on my head.

I don't know how long I was unconscious, but I came to on a table, looking up into my mother and daddy's faces, which were peering worriedly at me. There was another face I didn't know. It turns out that he was the x-ray technician.

This is my very first recollection of life, seeing my mother, in her white nurse's uniform, turning upside down as I went over the edge of the ramp, and then waking up to her face and daddy's face looking down at me on that table. That's the only thing I personally remember of that event. But Mother told me years later that she and Daddy were praying earnestly through that whole ordeal.

My skull was split open on the back of my head from ear to ear. Mother told me that the doctor predicted that I would have several problems throughout my life because of this type of injury, including seizures, vision loss, severe headaches and possibly even paralysis. Shortly after this, I started having a seizure, but Mother prayed and it stopped immediately, and I have never had one since. Nor have I experienced any of the other problems the doctor expected me to have. Again, God was in my life and He protected and healed me.

"For I will restore health unto thee, and I will heal thee of thy wounds, saith the LORD…" (Jer. 30:17, first part).

No Train

"Rita Kay! Rita Kay! Rita Kay!" my mother called frantically as she ran around the house looking in the bushes and searching the yard. Where had her three-year-old gone? She and I had been throwing a ball back and forth one afternoon in the front yard when the telephone rang. Mother ran inside to answer the phone, but the call took longer than she thought, and when she came tearing back outside to check on me I was already gone! Kitty and Puppy were gone also.

Mother prayed, "God, where is my little girl? Please keep her safe." Suddenly, it came to Mother's mind, THE TRAIN! Most days Mother took me through the woods, hand-in-hand, to the track on the other side to watch the train go by. Now, Mother realized that her little girl had gone in that direction, down the path, all by herself. Knowing I would not know to stay safely off the track,

Mother started running down the trail through the woods, praying constantly that she would make it to me in time.

Glancing at her watch, Mother realized with dread that it was time for the train. "Please, Lord, stop the train. Save my precious daughter." Having not yet heard the train, she presumed it was late. When she reached the track, she waited momentarily for the sound, her eyes searching diligently up and down the track. No little girl, no puppy, no kitty, AND no train. Hesitantly, Mother crossed the track and continued her frantic search down the trail through more woods. At that moment she realized that God had answered the first part of her prayer. God had truly stopped the train for it never came through there that day at all.

Running once more and praying, "Save my Rita Kay!" Mother came to the river, but she had no way to cross. Frantic, she looked down the river. No child. Then she looked up the river. No child. But wait! What was that on the bank in the distance? There were Puppy and Kitty lying on the bank watching something in the river! It was ME naively wading out into the rapid current, already chest deep in the water. Mother ran even faster down to where I was, waded out into the river, scooped me up, and safely brought me home, crossing over the track with still no train. God had also answered the second part of Mother's prayer: "Save my Rita Kay."

No one could figure out why a big, long freight train, that ran EVERY DAY at the same time, never came on that particular day.

"I sought the LORD, and he heard me, and delivered me from all my fears" (Ps. 34:4).

The next morning, the local newspaper reported about the strange fact that the train did not go through the day before. No one could figure out why a big, long freight train, that ran EVERY DAY at the same time, never came on that particular day.

Dear reader, you and I know why, don't we? God truly stopped that train in answer to a worried mother's prayer for her little daughter.

"And it shall come to pass, that before they call, I will answer; and while they are yet speaking, I will hear" (Isa. 65:24).

Uninvited Guests

When I was young and in elementary school, we lived on a lake in Florida. We did not have a clothes dryer, so mother used a nice, long clothes line outside in the back yard beside the house. Mother would put the newly washed and wet clothes in her laundry basket and go to the back door. Opening the door usually revealed three of our sunbathing backyard guests from the large lakes: alligators basking in the beautiful Florida sun, directly under the clothesline.

Not knowing the art of walking safely through sleeping eight-to-ten-foot long alligators, mother would yell and holler to awaken them in hopes that they would move—preferably back to the lake! The lounging reptiles would raise their gigantic heads, look toward Mother, and lay their heads back down again as if to say, "Oh, it's just her again; never mind ... everyone go back to sleep."

Mother finally decided to take drastic measures after time and again not being able to access her clothes line when she needed it because of those lazy alligators. One day when the yard was clear, and no alligators were present, Mother took her bucket out around the yard and driveway and gathered small rocks. The next washday Mother was prepared. She carried the basket of wet clothes through the back door and stopped at the top of the steps and looked at the alligators. She then set the basket down and picked up the bucket of rocks.

First she tried her normal wake-up tactics. As usual, the sleeping giants raised their heads to make sure it WAS the same intruder, but this time, as they attempted to continue their basking, they suddenly got pelted with rocks and words. Mother was shouting "Get away from the clothesline and let me hang up my clothes!"

"Hey, maybe she means it this time! Maybe we should go back to the water. It's safer there," the big, strong reptiles must have decided.

Ever so slowly, one by one, they roused, stretched their legs, and started their trek toward the lake. After many weeks of this, they finally concluded it would probably be better if they relocated their basking spot. Hence, they moved to the open field across from the clothesline, still bordering the lake. Mother had her clothesline back!

Thinking of mother not giving up the fight for her clothesline makes me think of my battle with my besetting sin: do I fight until I overcome it, or do I just give up and let it have its way and linger? I must have my ammunition ready and persevere until it's gone. God will help me! As big and strong and persistent as my besetting sin is, with God NOTHING is impossible.

"And Jesus said unto them, Because of your unbelief: for verily I say unto you, If ye have faith as a grain of mustard seed, ye shall say unto this mountain, Remove hence to yonder place; and it shall remove; and nothing shall be impossible unto you'" (Matt. 17:20).

Forgiveness

Two of Mother's sisters had not spoken to each other for over two years. This disturbed my mother very much. After praying about the tense situation, one day Mother invited her two wayward siblings to come to our house. Neither knew, of course, that the other was invited.

The older sister came first. Mother let her in and showed her to the couch. In a little while, the younger sister came to the door. Seeing her older sister, she threw her head in the air and turned away as she sat down. Each refused to look at the other as they sat on opposite ends of the couch.

Mother pulled a stool up to the center front of the couch and sat down, where she could face both sisters. Looking at the oldest one, she said, "Are you planning on going to heaven?"

The older sister answered, "Well, yes."

Then looking at the younger sister, Mother said, "Are you planning on going to heaven?"

A bit prissy, she answered, "But, of course!"

> *"Well ... in heaven we are going to get along. So, if we are NOT getting along here ... then ... SOMEBODY'S not going to go."*

Then, looking back and forth at each of their faces, Mother slowly and caringly said, "Well ... in heaven we are going to get along. So, if we are NOT getting along here ... then ... SOMEBODY'S not going to go."

Evidently neither sister had thought of that. Both their mouths dropped open as they stared for some time in astonishment at their middle sister. Then each one looked at the other and broke down weeping. Scooting across the empty space to the middle of the couch, they embraced each other saying, "I'm sorry."

"Being confident of this very thing, that he which hath begun a good work in you will perform it until the day of Jesus Christ" (Phil. 1:6).

Lost In London

What a thrilling day it was when I found out that my friend, Peggy, and I could go to Europe with a church group. We were so excited! We decided to pack our clothes together in one suitcase. This seemed easier because then, in the other suitcase, we could put things we would use up, like film for our camera, toilet paper, and personal items, which could then be replaced with souvenirs and we would still have plenty of room without taking extra luggage. I had the summer off from my rigorous college courses, and it was so much fun planning and packing for this trip of a lifetime!

At last the day came and off we flew to London, England, where we planned to spend our first few days. We were all lodging in the dormitory of a college that was closed for the summer. It was an inexpensive and convenient place for such a large group to stay. One day our church group came back from sightseeing at 5:00 pm and were planning to rest for the remainder of the afternoon and evening—the jet-lag and long day of touring seemed to be wearing everyone out except for Peggy and me. We were younger than most of the others and not yet ready for our day to end. I love meeting people and learning all I can about other cultures and countries. So, in one of my "brainy" moments, I made a suggestion to Peggy, "Let's go ride the double-decker buses for a while, then come back on the subway. We can meet and talk to the English people." Peggy thought that was a great idea. So, off we went!

We walked down a couple of blocks to a bus stop and got on the double-decker public transit bus for our ride. It was so much fun riding on the upper deck and talking to the precious English people with their "cute accents." After a while we switched over to the subway and started back toward where we were staying—or so we thought. Laughing and talking with the other passengers and seeing the beautiful lights as we came up out of the underground tunnels was delightful.

Suddenly, as we emerged from the tunnel, I realized that it was dark up there, too! I said, "Oh, Peggy, IT'S DARK! What time is it?!"

She looked at her watch, then almost shouted with surprise, "Oh my, it's eleven o'clock!"

Having so much fun, we had forgotten all about the time! *Wow, we thought, we better get off at the next station and get back to our room.* Climbing up the many steps from the subway, we came outside into a residential area that was totally dark except for an occasional street light.

Peggy started to cry. "Where are we?" she wailed, trying to hold back the tears. "We'll never find our way back to the dormitory!"

"Bold and brave" me, who had no fears, said, "Oh, of course we will. We'll just ask someone where the Pentland House is." The street was deserted except for a man walking on our side of the street toward us. Seeing a strange man walking toward you on a dark street could cause anxiety, but as he was passing us, I calmly asked, "could you please tell us where the Pentland House is?"

"Never heard of it," was the reply—and he kept on walking.

Soon a man and woman came walking up the street together. Bravely, I stepped up to them and asked, "Could you please tell me where the Pentland House is?" But again they had never heard of it. Peggy was still crying. I, on the other hand, continued to have all kinds of hope that someone would know where we were staying. After all, it couldn't be very far from here.

We then realized that, while we had been sure to remember the name of the dormitory we were staying in, we had failed to find out the name of the college itself, and there were many colleges in that metropolis!

I still thought that I had it all figured out; and I assured Peggy that we could ride the city bus back to our location—because the driver would surely know where we were supposed to be. Peggy finally stopped crying and started smiling, "Oh yes, that's what we'll do." So, to the next people that happened along, I asked the location of the nearest bus stop. They directed us to one about two blocks away.

As we walked around the last corner, we saw the bus stop sign under a street light. There were about eight people standing and waiting. Some were reading the newspaper by street light, while the others talked softly among themselves as they waited for the bus. Peggy and I took our places at the end of the line to wait with them. At that time the buses in London ran every fifteen minutes, and by then it was 11:30 p.m. As we waited, 11:45 came and went—then 12 midnight—then 12:15. Still no bus. What was wrong?

Peggy and I were standing facing each other talking when I saw over her shoulder, about a block and half down the street opposite from where we had come, a black Englishman crawling out from under the tall hedge that ran along the side walk He stood up straight, brushed himself off, looked up the street, then down the street, as if deciding which way to go! Then, with a decided jump, he started our way. I watched as he got closer, thinking he was probably going to take the bus, too.

Instead of getting in line behind us, he walked right up to us. Looking at me, he said, "Are you waiting for the bus?"

Determined not to speak to this stranger, I stuck my nose in the air and looked the other way.

As if he didn't notice, he said again, "Are you waiting for the bus?"

Disgustedly, trying to get rid of this "irritant," I put my hands on my hips and looked straight at him and sneered, "Of course we are waiting for the bus. What do you think we are standing here for? Our health?"

Totally oblivious to my hateful attitude, he said "The buses went on strike at 11:00."

Now, for the first time even I was horrified and felt like crying! I was thinking, *"What are we going to do?"* Stunned, I looked right into his face for the first time. I saw His face was radiant, and he had a peaceful look and a beautiful smile,

Looking at me, the man's beautiful smile never faltered as he said, "Where are you going?"

Very humbled, now, I replied, "Well, you have probably never heard of it. We are staying at the Pentland House."

His smile got even bigger as he said, "Yes, I've heard of it—it is clear across London.

Peggy and I looked at each other and she started crying again. Oh my! We thought, *how will we ever get there?!*

Then he said, sweetly, "I live two doors down from it. I am going to walk; do you want to walk with me?"

"Oh yes, yes we do," I said, regaining hope, while Peggy was nodding and smiling through her tears. Off we started, *back the way he had just come,* on our trek across the city of London.

The man (no longer a disgusting stranger) walked very fast. Sometimes I had to run a few steps to keep up. Peggy walked on one side and a humbled Rita was on the other side of this amazingly nice man. He also sang and had us singing with him as we walked and walked. He sang old hymns. The one he sang the most was, "Anywhere With Jesus I Can Safely Go."

Once, the kind man (I call him an angel, maybe even mine) looked at me as we hastened through the streets, and asked, "Do you know that Jesus is coming soon?" I nodded, and then he said, "Are you ready?"

We walked all the rest of the night, till suddenly he stopped and bowed toward us while gesturing his hand toward the gate of the Pentland House! We were home safe! Oh what joy! So now, I can say that I have walked all the way across London, singing! What a thrilling adventure!

I don't know for sure if he was an angel or not, but I do know without a doubt that he was from God.

Before either Peggy or I thought even to pray, God sent a man to help us.

"Thou wilt shew me the path of life: in Thy presence is fullness of joy; at Thy right hand there are pleasures for evermore" (Ps. 16:11).

Song: ANYWHERE WITH JESUS by Jessie Pounds

Verse 1:

Anywhere with Jesus I can safely go, Anywhere He leads me in this world below. Anywhere without Him, dearest joys would fade; Anywhere with Jesus I am not afraid.

CHORUS:

Anywhere! anywhere! Fear I cannot know. Anywhere with Jesus I can safely go.

Verse 2:

Anywhere with Jesus I am not alone, Other friends may fail me, He is still my own. Though His hand may lead me over dreary way, Anywhere with Jesus is a house of praise.

Verse 3:

Anywhere with Jesus I can go to sleep, When the darkening shadows round about me creep Knowing I shall waken never more to roam, Anywhere with Jesus will be home, sweet home.

Rumors

If it had not been the Lord who was on our side, when men rose up against us: then they had swallowed us up quick, when their wrath was kindled against us: then the waters had overwhelmed us, the stream had gone over our soul: then the proud waters had gone over our soul. Blessed be the Lord, Who hath not given us as a prey to their teeth. Our soul is escaped as a bird out of the snare of the fowlers: the snare is broken, and we are escaped. Our help is in the name of the Lord, who made heaven and earth. (Ps. 124: 2–8)

These Bible verses come to my mind as I sit on the back patio of our island home in Guam, watching the mighty waves of the Pacific Ocean. They peacefully swell larger and larger to big, blue whale size, then suddenly crash out, white billows rushing frantically upon the reef, just in time to be pulled back under more billowing waves. Other white-capped waves crash turbulently against the rugged cliffs that are protruding out past the reef, like soldiers standing taut to protect their domain. Sometimes it seems like I'm there in the turbulent water, trying to keep my head afloat, when I'm hit with another huge wave of the proud, raging water that tries to overwhelm me and cover me up.

That's the way I found my mother feeling one summer when I spent my college break with her in her new apartment. Mother and Daddy lived in Washington, DC, where they both worked, but Mother had taken some time off to go to another state to take care of her aging mother, my grandma. The first Sabbath morning I was there with her, I got up and began preparing to go to church. Mother, however, kept lying in bed. I fixed breakfast and called Mother to come eat.

She announced, "I don't go to church anymore."

Totally shocked, numbed, and confused, I sat down on the side of her bed. This precious, loving woman, who all my life always went to church—who taught ME to go to church and always made sure we were on time—NOW isn't going to church? How could that be?

As I sat there beside her, the whole story came out. It seemed that the neighborhood gossips started mouthing their assumptions as to why Mother and Daddy were now living in two different states. No one had bothered to ask her. They just assumed that Kate and Amos were separated and getting a divorce. Soon the baseless news was all over the community. If that wasn't enough, the various men around the area, both married and unmarried, started calling Mother for dates. That, in itself, nearly wiped her out. Of course, she was happily married—and she told them so.

But the rumors soared that Mother was "running around" with all of these men. When Mother would walk into church, the majority of the people, and even her "friends," would start their whispering to each other and turn their heads. In her mind, "the proud waters had gone over [her] soul." People "rose up against" her. They "had swallowed [her] up quick" and "their wrath was kindled against" her. She was so hurt, brokenhearted, and angry. She ended her story by saying, "and I don't want to be around those all-fired holy people—they think they are so good."

In my shock at such beastly actions I became angry. How could people who claim to be "Christians" and friends do such things? We whispered a prayer to God in heaven that calmed us both down. Then, through me, God spoke to both of us. "Mother, you have as much right to go to that church as anybody. Jesus wants you there. He loves you. He knows the truth. He knows the things they are saying are not true. Get up, let's get dressed, and walk into that church arm-in-arm, with our noses in the air. You don't have to speak to anyone if you don't want to. We will walk across the foyer together, and go into the sanctuary together, keeping our eyes straight ahead and on Jesus (behind the baptistery there is a large, beautiful stained-glass picture of Jesus). We will listen to the sermon, the message God has for us today. Then when it is over, we will walk out arm-in-arm and come home."

Mother was thrilled with this idea because she didn't like to miss church. We got dressed and did just that. As we walked into church that first time, people pulled away and whispered to each other. But I kept Mother's arm tightly in mine and pulled gently as we walked through the people to the sanctuary. The sermon was beautiful and just what we needed. As soon as it was over, we got up, went out, and headed back home. We did this each week for the first part of the summer. After a few weeks, people started speaking to us. They actually started hugging Mother and telling her they were glad to see her.

> *As we walked into church that first time, people pulled away and whispered to each other.*

Mother was again going to church on a regular basis and loving it. Some people apologized to her, but others did not. She didn't care for she forgave all of them, as Jesus would want her to do. She was just thankful to have her friends back and to be able to go to church again.

"Our help is in the name of the Lord Who made heaven and earth" (Ps. 124:8).

God is faithful and keeps His promises.

Through The Valley Of Death

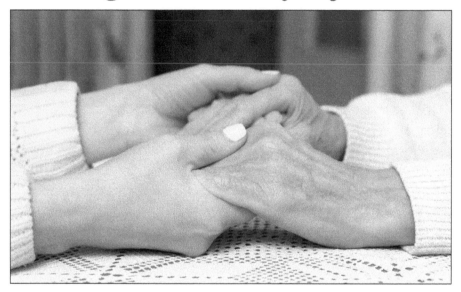

My mother and I were very close in my growing-up years. We even dressed alike and did lots of fun things together.

She was a registered nurse and worked to help sick people get well. Other than a ruptured appendix, she herself was never sick. So, when we got word that she had cancer, I wasn't too worried at first, because I thought "she will be able to get over this, too, and will come out on top." She had never been a patient in the hospital except for that ruptured appendix and my birth.

I had gotten married the year before her diagnosis and lived in a different state. I went home and stayed with her as much as I could while she underwent radiation and, as I thought, got well.

One day as I sat at her bedside watching her sleep, the thought occurred to me, "What if she doesn't get well?" Panic struck me and I had to run from the room to keep from waking her with my sobs. I started praying (which I should have been doing all along) that God would heal her. I added, however, "But if she doesn't get well, then, please, help me know what to do."

The thought of living without my mother to call me long distance every Monday morning and say, "Good morning, Sugar, I love you. Whatcha gonna do, today?" overwhelmed me. To think that I wouldn't be able to call HER anytime and ask whether or not to "put salt in homemade applesauce" was more than I could handle.

I started praying, "God if my mother is REALLY going to die, please help our last moments together to be special." Then He brought to my mind these things to pray for:

1. Please give me something to say to her that she will understand and that will bring peace to her in her last moments.

2. Please help me to be with her when she dies.

3. Please help her to die with a smile on her face so I'll know she is at peace.

4. Please help her to go in her sleep so she won't suffer.

Even though I still really didn't think she would die, I continued to pray for these same four things every day. I told no one of my prayers.

A few days after I started praying, Mother wanted to get up and come to the table for breakfast. While she and I ate what turned out to be our last meal at the table together, she said, "You know, I had the strangest dream the other night."

I responded, "What did you dream?" I am not a dream interpreter, but God put into my mind what Mother's dream meant as she related it to me.

Mother said, "Well, I was in an airplane with lots of other people and we were flying over water. The water was black and all around the plane was black. I couldn't see the water, but I knew it was down there. I couldn't see anything outside of the plane except straight ahead in the distance where there were beautiful lights of all colors. We were flying straight toward the beautiful lights. Isn't that a strange dream?"

"Well, maybe it's not so strange," I observed. "See, you were in the airplane flying—maybe meaning swiftness and maybe your illness will be fast. (I was thinking she would get well soon). You were flying over water. Water in the Bible symbolizes people (Rev. 17:15). The black waters and the darkness all around could mean the sin, toil, and strife of this world and the fact that you are moving rapidly means that you will miss a lot of it. The beautiful lights of all colors that you were flying toward could be the New Jerusalem (heaven) with its twelve shining foundations (Rev. 21:14, 19, 20), brilliant walls, and gates of pearl (Rev. 21:21). Maybe the light from God is reflecting on the beautiful stones and shining out in all colors (Rev. 21:23)."

What a wonderful gift God gave us when He sent her that dream and showed me the meaning of it— we BOTH had a new peace about the future that we hadn't had before.

The most beautiful smile came over Mother's face as she said, "So, maybe I don't have long to suffer—maybe I will just go to sleep (Eph. 5:14, John 11:11, 14) and sleep through all of the troubles that are still to come on this earth. When Jesus comes, He will wake me up and I will get to go with Him, my family, friends, and all that love Him to heaven where the beautiful lights are!" (1 Thess. 4:16–18).

Until that moment, Mother would cry if anyone spoke of her dying, and there was no way I would even mention it! I couldn't accept the dreadful thought myself. What a wonderful gift God gave us when He sent her that dream and showed me the meaning of it—we BOTH had a new peace about the future that we hadn't had before.

The next day, Mother was weaker. The second day after our "dream conversation," Mother asked me to play her favorite song on the piano— "Always Cheerful" by Fanny Crosby. I looked for the music and found it had four sharps. Never in my life had I played anything with four sharps; in fact, I had never even played "Always Cheerful" before. It was one of the songs Mother had sung to me as a child while rocking me to sleep. As I got older and we sang the song together, she herself accompanied us on the piano. Even though four sharps and a never-played-before piece were far from my comfort zone, Mother had asked specifically for that song. So, I sat there at the piano staring at the music. Mother was in the next room waiting to hear her song.

Again I prayed, "God, please help me to play this once for my dear mother." In faith I put my hands on the keyboard and started to play ... and I played through the whole song! Mother was thrilled and weakly sang along. When we were through, I could not play it again—I've not been able to play that arrangement with the four sharps since.

That night at 9:00, I kissed Mother good night and we prayed together. Two hours and forty-five minutes later, I was down on my knees saying my own prayer, when Someone (I couldn't see anyone) took my arm, lifted me up, and led me around to Mother. I sat down on the side of her bed and took her left arm and hand onto my lap. She was sleeping so peacefully. Then suddenly she started to cry in her sleep. I leaned over to her and said, "Don't cry, Mother—remember the beautiful lights? You are almost there!" Mother stopped crying and smiled, then took her last three breaths, and died at 11:50 p.m.

There is no way I would have ever been able to face this without God working things out like He did. He answered <u>all four</u> of my prayers for my mother that He Himself impressed me to pray, and she fell asleep in Him with a beautiful, heaven-sent peace.

God doesn't just half-way do things—I've learned that time and again. This time, He did one more special thing for me with my mother. At the funeral home, I was taken to see her; I reached down to kiss her cheek and touch her arms. Her left arm (The one I had been holding when she died) was still perfectly warm. That made it all so very special for me.

The God of the universe, Who keeps the stars and sun in place, the earth and moon in rotation, is our awesome God and cares *all* about even the *little things* in our lives!!! Mother has no more worries, fear, or pain. She is sleeping peacefully, now, in her grave, until Jesus comes. I am so thankful that He will awaken her and call her up out of the grave along with all who have died loving Him, to take them and all the living that love Him to live with Him forever. I keep looking toward that day.

"Yea, though I walk through the valley of the shadow of death, I will fear no evil, for Thou art with me; Thy rod and Thy staff, they comfort me" (Ps. 23:4).

Song: ALWAYS CHEERFUL by Fanny Crosby

Verse 1:

Let our hearts be always cheerful; Why should murm'ring enter there, When our kind and loving Father Makes us children of His care?

CHORUS:

Always cheerful always cheerful, Sunshine all around we see; Full of beauty is the path of duty, Cheerful we may always be.

Verse 2:

With His gentle hand to lead us, Should the pow'rs of sin assail, He has promised grace to help us; Never can His promise fail. [Chorus]

Verse 3:

When we turn aside from duty, Comes the pain of doing wrong; And a shadow, creeping o'er us, Checks the rapture of our song. [Chorus]

Verse 4:

Oh! the good are always happy, And their path is ever bright; Let us heed the blessed counsel, Shun the wrong and love the right. [Chorus]

Snake

When my son, Dallas, was three-years-old, we lived in Nashville, Tennessee. In our morning family worships we had learned how important it is to obey and to obey quickly.

> **Dallas ran straight to me. The snake was already in striking distance**

Some days, living in the city, we needed to go to a place of peace and quiet, so I found a park with a section of woods. Knowing Dallas would love walking in the woods, I took him early one morning to that park. Together, we started up a wooded path. The brisk, morning air gave Dallas lots of energy to run—much faster than his mother! At the top of the small hill sat a bench under the trees. I made myself comfortable on that bench to allow Dallas time to play in the dirt with the small sticks he always had with him.

Presently, to my horror, I saw a snake come slowly slithering out of the woods behind Dallas, winding its way straight toward him! Realizing that there wasn't enough time for me to run across the path and grab Dallas, I said to him very sternly, "Dallas! Come to Mommy NOW!" Immediately, Dallas ran straight to me. The snake was already in striking distance of Dallas, but it hadn't coiled yet. If Dallas had hesitated, it could have struck him. Grabbing up my precious three-year-old, I turned and showed him the snake and then ran down the path out of the woods.

Over and over, I have thanked God that my children learned to obey *immediately* when I called. I pray that I, their mother, will always obey God in the same way!

"…it may be well with us when we obey the voice of the Lord our God" (Jer. 42:6, last part).

Little Red Ball

When Dallas was three years old, he put a quarter in a ball machine. When he turned the knob, he got back a pretty red ball, about an inch in diameter. Dallas loved his new little ball that kept bouncing higher and higher, and he would bounce it all over the house.

One day, he and I were going to take a lunch and go to our favorite park and play—this is the same park where we saw the snake in the previous story. Dallas came into the kitchen where I was making our lunch to take that morning and asked, "Mommy, can I take my new red ball to the park?"

I said, "No, honey, it's too small and you might lose it if you take it outside."

"Oh, Mommy, *please,* may I take it? Please, please, please!"

I continued to say "no."

A while later, my little son came back, saying, "Mommy, I promise I will take good care of my new red ball and won't lose it. PLEASE let me take it."

Finally relenting, I responded, "Okay, you may take it to the park, but on condition that you keep it in your pocket. You MUST keep it in your pocket."

"Okay, Mommy," he said excitedly and began jumping and playing happily throughout the house, bouncing his ball and singing, "I get to take my ball, I get to take my ball!"

Arriving at the park, I reminded him, "Keep your new ball in your pocket so you won't lose it."

He showed me the ball in his pocket as he said, "Okay, Mommy."

We played on the jungle gym, the teeter-totters, the swings, merry-go-round, and the other fun things there. Then it was time to eat. I took Dallas to a grassy area where we could spread our blanket. I said, "Wait right here while I get our lunch from the car." The car wasn't far, so I could keep my eyes on him and be sure he didn't wander off.

When I got back to the grassy area, Dallas was crying. Quickly, I knelt down and put my arm around him, as I asked, "Dallas, honey, what's the matter?" I was looking around for a snake, sharp object, or anything that could have made him cry.

"Oh, Mommy," he sobbed, "I disobeyed you. I took my ball out of my pocket to just bounce it once, *just once*, and now it's gone!" Then he sobbed even more.

I hugged him as I said, "Well, let's look for it." So we looked, and looked, and looked, in every direction. Over this way, over that way, the other way. You would think that a red ball down in green grass would be easy to spot, but that wasn't the case. We ran our hands through the grass and even walked with our bare feet, thinking that maybe we could feel it with our toes. But try as we might, we could *not* find his new ball.

Finally, after some time, little Dallas looked up at me and, through his tears, said, "Mommy, can we ask Jesus? He knows where it is."

I Hadn't even thought of that yet myself. Of course I said, "Why, yes, honey, let's ask Him."

So my three-year-old Dallas and I knelt down right there in the grass, closed our eyes, folded our hands, and little sobbing Dallas prayed, "Dear Jesus, I'm sorry I disobeyed Mommy; please help me find my ball. Amen."

We opened our eyes and to my surprise, right there, about two feet in front of us, was the red ball sitting on TOP of the green grass!

Oh, for the faith of a child!

"But Jesus said, Suffer little children, and forbid them not, to come unto me: for of such is the kingdom of heaven" (Matt. 19:14).

Hungry In Nashville

My son Dallas was three-years-old and a happy little boy, full of energy, and so very hungry at meal times. Unfortunately, at this time our income had come to an abrupt halt since my husband had left us for a time. Sometime later, I became aware that we were getting low on food. I took stock of our refrigerator, and discovered to my disappointment, that we had only half-a-loaf of bread and half-a-jar of mayonnaise in the whole refrigerator! When I opened the pantry door, I almost said out loud, "Where's the food?" There was one rolled package of round crackers and one can of pickled green beans. I then asked myself, "Why did I buy pickled green beans? I never even liked them." But now, with nothing else in the pantry, I was very thankful for them. "I'll save these for Sabbath," I told myself, "So it will be a special meal for our special day."

I checked my purse for money to buy some groceries, but, oh! I only had one dollar, and we were out of toilet paper, too. Now what to do? Spend my last dollar for food or for toilet paper?

Since the mayonnaise was what we had the most of, I put it real thick on both pieces of bread, with one layer of crackers between to make a cracker sandwich for Dallas and the same for me. Talk about good! We loved them, so we ate one cracker sandwich a day as long as the bread held out.

To get a three-year-old boy to be happy with one meal a day, I would pull him in bed with me when he awakened in the morning and sing to him, tell him stories, and anything to keep his mind from thinking "hungry." Then he would go back to sleep. When he woke up again, it was close to noon, so we would get up and would eat our delicious cracker sandwich.

I began praying, asking God what to do to feed my son and me. That night there was a knock on the door. I opened it and there stood a friend of the family with *two grocery bags full of food*. Since I had not told anyone of our dilemma, I asked this friend, "How did you know?" He answered that God had impressed him that we needed food."

He set the two bags down on the table and Dallas climbed up and began taking everything out one at a time, excitedly exclaiming, "Mommy, this is like Christmas!"

> *"God, if You will feed my little boy, I will never, ever waste another bite of food."*

The friend could see that we were so happy. We thanked him over and over.

"They shall hunger no more, neither thirst anymore; neither shall the sun light on them, nor any heat. For the Lamb which is in the midst of the throne shall feed them, and shall lead them unto living fountains of waters: and God shall wipe away all tears from their eyes" (Rev. 7:16–17).

A few weeks later, still without money and not being able to pay our rent, we got evicted. The landlord, thankfully, gave us two weeks to find another place. A friend knew a lady with a basement apartment. After the arrangements were made, we moved from our three-bedroom house to the small one-bedroom apartment. But, as He always does, God made a blessing out of this, too! Our small apartment had a back patio overlooking the Cumberland River. That's where we started eating our breakfasts every morning, watching the boats on the river, and thanking God for His loving kindness to us.

Not long after, our food supply ran out again. This time I prayed, "God, if You will feed my little boy, I will never, ever waste another bite of food." Suddenly and miraculously, food came to us from various sources. God kept our food supply coming. As God kept up His end of the bargain, so must I keep my end of the bargain. To this day, I've tried to never waste any food or throw it away.

"Blessed be the Lord, Who daily loadeth us with benefits, even the God of our salvation" (Ps. 68:19).

Baseball Bat Peace

When my husband returned we moved to North Carolina where he got a job driving an eighteen-wheeler across country. When he was on these road trips I thought that now it was up to me to protect my children (we now had two) and all our house and property. My husband would be gone anywhere from one week to six weeks. I finally figured out that the best defense—at least for me—against someone breaking into our house was to keep a baseball bat ready at my bedside just in case I needed to protect myself and my children from an intruder. Every night after getting the children to bed I would say a quick prayer for safety and get ready for bed myself.

Just as I would doze off to sleep, there would be a noise somewhere in the house. That was my cue—I just knew for sure that someone was breaking in. So, I jumped up, grabbed my baseball bat, swung it over my shoulder, and tip toed quietly down the hall toward the living room.

Now my dilemma that I discovered the first night was this: the front door was on one side of the living room to my left as I came down the hall. Unfortunately, the back door was the other direction through the dining room, and about the same distance from the hall as the front door. To my horror, I couldn't tell whether the sound of someone breaking in was at the front or the back! This meant that when I got to the end of the hall at the living room, if I looked left at the front door, it could be that the intruder would come from the back door in the other direction. He could come from behind and clobber ME over the head while I was looking at the front door. The same thing could happen if I checked the back door first and the intruder came from the front. All of this came to me as I made my first trek down the hall to "protect" my sleeping children.

Desperately, I decided that I would do one of those speed looks—looking both directions very rapidly. This is the kind of movement that sprains your neck and gives you a dizzy headache. Still, I succeeded in the plan, and much to my amazement, there were no intruders at the front OR back doors. Both doors were still locked, too!

Walking back down the hall with my bat and my new headache, I crawled into bed, only to hear another sound. This one was definitely an intruder! I just knew it! So, up again and down the hall with my ever-present baseball bat. This nightly action went on for several weeks. I was losing sleep, stressed with fright and worry, and add to that the unnatural neck action, and I was left in a tired frenzy.

One night, after my usual noise-attending actions, I crawled back into bed exhausted and crying. Right then the thought came to my mind, "Hey, I claim to be a Christian! That's got to count for something!" So, right then and there I prayed out loud: "God, if you are here and taking care of us, help me to know it." That very instant, the most beautiful, peaceful feeling filled my whole room. It was simply fantastic! I had never known such peace before.

God filled our whole house that night with a peace unlike I had ever known. And that peace has been in this house ever since—

at least forty years and counting! We have never been afraid of intruders, or anything in this house since then. God is so awesome! He truly takes care of us.

"I laid me down and slept; I awaked; for the LORD sustained me" (Ps. 3:5).

The Wood Stove

Living in the mountains is such a beautiful luxury! Well, except if you don't know anything about building fires! Our house in the Appalachian Mountains of North Carolina had no heat source except a cast-iron, pot-bellied wood stove. My husband was very good at starting the fires in the stove to keep us warm, so we were always toasty.

That is, we were toasty warm until he started driving an eighteen-wheeler truck and being gone from home more and more often. I was used to "city-living" where all you had to do was adjust the thermostat on the wall to warm or cool the house. No Problem!

He had tried to show me how to start the fire. First you put wadded up newspaper, then tiny kindling, then a bit bigger kindling, then, when the fire starts burning, you can put on bigger wood. For some reason that plan did not work for me back then. I did exactly like he said, but the paper burned up and the flame went out.

Every morning I would get up and attempt to start a fire. My two small children would wake up and want to get up, too. So, I would carry them to the living room couch to keep their feet off the cold floor, wrap them in blankets to keep them warm, and give them books to look at while I tried to start the fire.

This particular morning, I had done everything my husband had taught me to do, but the fire was again NOT cooperating! The familiar adage, "Where there's smoke, there's fire," was not true in my wood stove. We sure had lots of smoke coming from those paper wads—but no fire. My precious little children, ages six and one, were bundled up on the couch looking at books to keep them from getting down and running across the cold floor. Six-year-old Dallas, just learning to read, was doing his very best to entertain his little sister, Katy. As they were shivering and shaking, he read as best he could, using the pictures to tell the stories.

Meanwhile, across the room at the stove, no progress was being made. The paper would burn up and go out, leaving the tiny kindling and bigger wood just sitting there smoldering. The inside of the stove was totally black. After three hours of lighting paper and kicking the stove I started crying because we were so cold—the thermometer in the hall read forty degrees. I was totally frustrated. Finally, in desperation, I looked up, crying, and prayed out loud: "God, if You are here and want us to get warm, please start this fire."

Immediately, the fire blazed up so hot, the room—the whole 20 x 16-foot room—was warm instantly. The children across the room on the couch were taking off their blankets. There was none of the regular wood-heat syndrome where the room would gradually get warm as the heat progressed across it. That whole room went from forty degrees to seventy-five degrees in less than a minute.

God is so awesome! He rules the whole universe and still cares if we are warm in the winter. He has been starting our wood stove fires ever since!

AND, HE PUTS THEM OUT, TOO!

One cold winter day, Dallas was at school, Katy was asleep in her crib, and I was in the bedroom at the opposite end of the house when I caught a whiff of metal burning. I ran down the hall into the living room to check the wood stove and found the fire blazing strongly.

The normally black stove pipe was totally red and crackling! I closed all the dampers, but the fire raged on, hotter and hotter. There was nothing I could do to put it out. If it didn't stop, it could catch the insulation in the attic on fire and burn the house down.

Frantically, I said, "Oh, Please God, put this fire out." Suddenly, out of nowhere, rain poured down the chimney and smothered the fire! As soon as the fire was out, the rain stopped. Don't you just love God? Isn't He awesome?!

"Thus saith the Lord, In an acceptable time have I heard thee, and in a day of salvation have I helped thee: and I will preserve thee..." (Isa. 49:8, first part).

The Flying Shoe

My children and I were driving home late one beautiful afternoon from getting our pictures made professionally. We were all dressed up from head-to-toe in our very best. Two-year-old Katy was asleep lying across the back seat of our car, while seven-year-old Dallas had fallen asleep stretched out in the front seat, and both his feet were sticking about a foot out of the window. As we drove along the two-lane road, suddenly one of Dallas' shoes blew off! Oh dear! What to do? He only had that one pair of church shoes and I had no money to buy more at that time.

With traffic so congested, it took a bit of time to find a spot to pull off the road. I glanced back at Katy. Neither child had awakened—even Dallas whose shoe was sucked off of his foot! I cautiously jumped out of the car, dodging the traffic, and ran back to where I thought the shoe might have landed, but I couldn't find it. It wasn't run over in the street, it wasn't in the ditch, and it wasn't on the bank. That black dress shoe was nowhere to be seen. I prayed, "Please, Lord, help me to find Dallas' shoe."

Very distraught and wondering what he could wear for church for the next few weeks, I hurried back to the car to check on my sleeping children.

Very distraught and wondering what he could wear for church for the next few weeks, I hurried back to the car to check on my sleeping children. As I came up from the back of the car, I could see the feet of Dallas, one with a shoe and one without, still hanging out the window. His feet weren't moving, so I knew he was still asleep. I glanced in the back window to make sure Katy was okay. Katy was still sound asleep, and there, lying on Katy's tummy, big enough to fill her whole chest, was Dallas' dress shoe. The shoe was heavy for the chest of a little two-year-old. If it had blown there and landed with any impact, it would have hurt her, or at least awakened her. It was more like the shoe had been set there gently … possibly by an angel.

I set the shoe on the floor and drove home. The children woke up as we turned into the driveway. Neither knew anything about the missing shoe nor the presence of another "Being."

"Commit thy way unto the LORD; trust also in him; and he shall bring it to pass" (Ps. 37:5).

The Hand

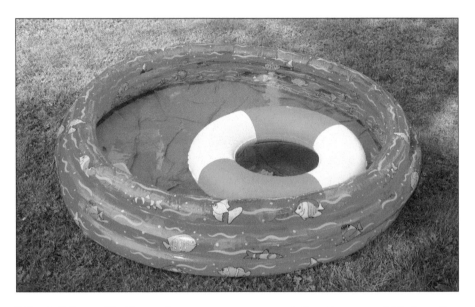

My children, Dallas, who was age seven at the time, and Katy, who was two, were so very excited to have a brand-new wading pool of their very own. They called it their "swimming pool."

At that time our home water pressure wasn't very strong. That would make even such a small pool difficult to fill, so we decided we could fill the pool with rain water instead, since it rained most every afternoon. To collect the water faster, Dallas found as many big, plastic containers as he could to catch the water that was coming off the corners of the roof. I donated all my large Tupperware® containers to the "pool cause." However, there was one massive, dripping area that had no container.

After searching unsuccessfully all over the house and garage for one more plastic container, I finally gave in to using a glass one. It was a gallon jug with a handle. I placed it under the drip myself, forgetting that when it was full that I would need to empty it into the pool since the glass was heavy and could break. I went back into the house and left the children in the warm summer rain, joyfully emptying container after container into their pool. I could hear the giggling and laughing from inside where I was working.

Suddenly there was a crash and then a scream. I ran as fast as I could down the hall, through the living room, and out the front door. There in the pouring rain, the porch and front door were already covered in blood. My little boy was getting up off of that gallon glass grape juice jug, which had been broken to pieces!

He had picked up the jug to empty it and slid on the wet porch, falling on top of the glass jug. The jug burst with the sharp point aimed toward his heart, but his right hand had gotten in the way, and instead of the point stabbing his heart, it stabbed and ripped the artery in his wrist, severing all the nerves and tendons to his fingers. The cut curved around the thumb in the palm and across his wrist. The blood was squirting about four feet into the air!

In first aid classes, the first thing they teach is to NOT PANIC. But I panicked—that was my baby bleeding! God then took over, kept me calm, and put the right thoughts in my mind, because I would never have been able to think straight in my panic. I pulled Dallas' hand down toward his wrist to stop the bleeding and wrapped a clean white dish cloth around it. Then I loaded him and his little sister, all dripping wet, into the car and called the emergency room in Fletcher, North Carolina, near where we lived, so they would be ready for him.

After the smaller, local hospital determined that they could not handle this severe case, the doctor called ahead and sent Dallas to the large regional hospital's emergency room, about twenty miles away in Asheville. This hospital was very efficient. When we walked through that emergency room door, a nurse immediately ushered us back to a room where a hand surgeon was already waiting for us. He looked the hand and wrist over, and then, while the nurses were getting little Dallas ready, the doctor came to me with pen and paper and drew a diagram and explained exactly what all he would have to do in micro surgery.

All the nerves to the hand had been severed. He would use a very long tweezer-like instrument to pull one nerve at a time back to the hand and sew it back to the other end of each nerve. He explained that in the five hours from the accident to the time of the surgery, the cut hand nerves had drawn all the way back to the elbow. They now had to be pulled—one at a time—back and sewn to the one they were severed from. The doctor also explained, "It's *humanly impossible* to match the nerves up exactly. Therefore," he demonstrated on my hand, "there will be several places where you touch here (the palm) but he will feel it there (under the little finger) or in a different place on his hand."

I thought right then: "I'm going to pray about that." I couldn't imagine God remaking something only half-way. The God I serve does a complete job!

Then, that very nice surgeon told me, "This surgery will take at least three hours. That is time for you to find somewhere for your little girl to stay tonight and get your things and come back. Plan to spend tonight here with your son." I was so thankful for that advice. I wouldn't have thought of any of that in the state of mind I was in. Again, God was there using other people to help me.

> *I couldn't imagine God remaking something only half-way. The God I serve does a complete job!*

The nurses had Dallas all ready for x-ray and then surgery. He was already drowsy from the anesthesia, so had stopped crying. I kissed him as they took him down the hall on the stretcher. He never even knew I left the hospital. My little Katy and I drove the twenty miles back toward home.

About one-and-a-half miles from home, my mental trauma hit. I started hyperventilating. My hands drew closed, making it hard to hold the steering wheel. I began exercising them one at a time—open/close/open/close—to try to make it home. Katy leaned over the front seat doing her little hand the same way, saying, "Mommy, what's this?" as she showed me her little hand doing the same thing. This made me laugh, which helped for a couple of minutes. But as we rounded a curve, I fainted over onto the passenger seat. As I went over, my foot slammed on the brake and I hit the gearshift which miraculously passed "Reverse" and the other gears and landed in

"Park." Our car evidently stopped in the middle of the road. It DID NOT go over the side and down to a creek that was there. Since I had fainted, I don't know what all happened then, but when I came to, two of my aunts were there. One of them was talking sweetly to Katy, getting her out of the back seat. My other aunt was trying to awaken me. Come to find out, they were in the FIRST car to come over the hill and find us there in the middle of the road. This was another of God's arrangements to protect my little girl and me. One of them kept Katy that night while the other helped me get my things together and drove me back to the hospital. I was there when Dallas came out of surgery and I stayed right by his side all night.

The next morning we both had a super surprise. His daddy, who had been out of town and could not be located through all this ordeal, walked into the room where we were. We were both delighted that he came. Again, God's providence came through.

When I took Dallas to the surgeon for his first checkup after the surgery, he still had the big cast on, covering his whole right hand up to his elbow. This was when the doctor reminded me of "the rest of the story." He said, "In two months, when we take the cast off, we will check his hand reflexes, touching in different places with this pointed instrument. I will tell you now—it is humanly impossible to match the nerves up exactly."

I had been praying to God for His providence in this matter all this time, and during the next two months, I prayed still, "God, You made that hand to start with; please make it again just like you did to begin with."

During the two months of having a cast on his right hand, Dallas learned to print and do all his functions with his left hand. Thankfully, school had been let out for the summer on the Friday before the accident on Monday. To me, that was just another sign of Providence.

Finally, the awaited day came. So many friends, relatives, and whole churches had been praying, and everyone now sat in suspense awaiting our phone call after the doctor's visit. The doctor was gracious, kind, and hopeful himself. He cut off the cast from Dallas' hand. It looked the same as before except for a big scar. Then the nurse held Dallas' hand while the doctor gently poked with the sharp instrument.

"Now, Dallas," he said as he poked. "Where do you feel this?"

Dallas said, "I feel it right where you are poking."

Over and over, the doctor tested the reflexes of that hand. Miraculously, each time it was felt right where it was poked! Doctor, nurses, Dallas, his mother, all of us were ecstatic!

I said, excitedly, "GOD DID IT!"

The doctor looked at me with a twinkle in his eye and said, "Well, I like to think Dallas had a good doctor, too."

I said, "Of course! GOD USED YOU to do it!" He smiled and nodded in agreement.

All of Dallas' hand was normal except for two things. The first was the scar. The second was that his thumb hung down. When you hold your hand relaxed with palm up, your fingers curve slightly and your thumb is up above the palm. Well, when Dallas held his right hand up like that, his thumb flopped down backwards below the palm.

This was in August. The doctor said, "I will give his thumb two months, till October fifteen, to correct itself. If it doesn't correct in that time, I will go back in there with more surgery and take a tendon from each finger (they have two apiece, and don't need them both) and put it in his thumb to help it work better." At this point, Dallas couldn't use his thumb at all.

Well, there again, all the friends, relatives, and churches were called. Again, I prayed, "God, You made his thumb to start with; please make it again." I never believed that fingers don't need both of their tendons. Our bodies need everything God put in them! It might function, but changing something that God did would weaken it from its original purpose!

Dallas started school that year using his left hand to write and to hold things. He also taught himself how to hold a lot of things with his four fingers on his right hand. I had marked October fifteen on the calendar to remember the proposed surgery, but I was praying otherwise.

I was in the kitchen on October eight when Dallas walked in saying, "Mommy, look!" I turned to see Dallas holding up his right hand, moving his thumb up and down in total control! Ecstatic again and so very thankful to God, we rushed back to the office to show the doctor. Again, God worked a miracle for everybody to see His love for all of us.

"Call unto me, and I will answer thee, and show thee great and mighty things, which thou knowest not" (Jer. 33:3).

Woods Sitting

If anyone ever says something positive about my children, I always tell them, "God raised my children, because I didn't know what I was doing. They don't come with instructions, you know!! I'm so thankful to Him for all He taught me and them."

One day, when they were small, God gave me the idea to sit in the woods quietly and to just wait to see what happens. So, I explained to them beforehand that we were going outside to sit still and quiet for five minutes and then quietly get up and not say a word till we got back into the house.

So the three of us went into the woods behind our house. We sat down on the ground, side-by-side, and didn't move, except to breathe, of course. Then I motioned when five minutes was up and we quietly came back into the house.

The children were excited and talking up a storm: "Did you see the bushy caterpillar crawl across my shoe?" "Mommy, that pretty ladybug landed on my arm! Did you see the little bird hop right up beside me?". Two or three times a week we would go out ... first ten minutes, then fifteen minutes. Soon the children wanted to be independent and sit alone! So I put Katy in one place, Dallas in another place, and I sat where I could see them both. Eventually, we got up to a whole hour of sitting still and quietly observing God's nature.

Each time when we got back into the house, they were bubbling over with new stories. Even little birds would hop up to them as they sat totally still. Thanks to God, the children learned valuable lessons there in nature.

One thing they learned was that there IS a time to be quiet and sit still! That helped over and over in their growing up years, and they learned if they are patient, better things happen.

"Be still, and know that I am God: I will be exalted among the heathen, I will be exalted in the earth" (Ps. 46:10.)

The Garden Spot

After we moved to the North Carolina mountains, we planted a garden. Our garden was rectangle, approximately fifty feet across both ends and 100 feet lengthwise. The dirt was excellent and we put compost on it throughout the fall and winter. We also had a beautiful, perfectly shaped, weeping willow tree growing at the edge of the yard. As the tree grew and grew over the years, part of its roots grew underground and into the upper corner of the garden.

The garden was at a perfect slope for drainage, helping all the vegetables to grow well. But, as the willow tree flourished, and the tree roots used the moisture, that upper quarter of the garden stayed dry all the time. This meant that the upper part of the garden quit producing vegetables. Each year it got worse and worse, until absolutely nothing would grow in that part of the garden.

When Dallas was eight, his teacher in Primary Class at church talked to the children about how to raise money for "Investment."

Investment is earning money for mission projects by donating all the proceeds of a project to God. She gave the children some ideas, like working for the neighbors in the yard, washing dishes, raking leaves, growing a garden, and selling your vegetables. That Sabbath, after we got home from church, Dallas asked, "Mommy, can I have part of our garden to grow vegetables for Investment?"

> *There, on his knees in the grass, with his little hands folded and head bowed toward his garden, was Dallas praying.*

My first thought was, "No, we need the garden for our own food." Then I remembered that upper part of the garden where nothing grows. I said, "Yes, you can have the upper part of the garden." I figured that whatever grew and matured to whatever size, he would be happy with. What I didn't know was that my little boy had a relationship with God—an inside connection, you might say—but I was soon going to learn.

He was delighted! The next day, we sat down and planned out his garden. He wanted to have cucumbers, squash, carrots, and radishes. The following day we set to work. The garden had already been plowed, so I showed him how to lay off his four short rows so they would be straight, and how to plant the seed. Then we gently covered them and marked the rows to show which vegetables were in which row.

Later that day I couldn't find Dallas anywhere. I looked out of the window toward his garden area and there, on his knees in the grass, with his little hands folded and head bowed toward his garden, was Dallas praying. He was asking Jesus to help his garden grow. Many times through that growing season, whenever I couldn't find my son, I looked out that window and there he was kneeling beside his/God's garden, praying.

Seeing my little boy on his knees in the grass praying for his new garden made me realize how selfish I had been for not being willing to share my garden with my son to do God's work. I felt terrible! I asked God to forgive me, which He did, and to help me never to be that way again.

God promises, "If we confess our sins, He is faithful and just to forgive us our sins, and to cleanse us from all unrighteousness" (1 John 1:9).

Well, when it was time to harvest our gardens, guess what? I probably don't need to tell you that my son's 8 x 15-foot plot of ground, where no edible food had grown for years, grew the largest, most luscious, and beautiful vegetables ever grown in that whole garden. The squash and cucumbers were the biggest and most tender I had ever seen. The radishes and carrots were huge and perfect in shape.

My dear little boy proudly picked his and God's vegetables, loaded them into his big red wagon, and pulled it to the neighbors who were delighted to buy them from him. He was so happy to be working for Jesus. My precious, God-trusting son took his earnings to his teacher at the church the next Sabbath to give for Investment. His teacher told me later that was the most money brought for Investment of the whole class.

God truly blessed the garden spot project and a little boy's faith—and taught his mommy a good lesson.

"Verily I say unto you, Whosoever shall not receive the kingdom of God as a little child, he shall not enter therein" (Mark 10:15).

Lake Keys

My two children and I went to the lake to spend the day. Our plan was to ride the paddle boats in the morning, at noon to eat our fun lunch that we brought, and then play on the playground equipment in the afternoon. We arrived at the park in the middle of the morning, put everything in the trunk of our car, including our lunch and my handbag, keeping out the car keys and only enough money for the paddle boats. After paying, I helped each child put on their lifejacket and climb into the paddle boat at the end of the long dock. Then I stepped into the boat myself. As I worked and wiggled myself around to the back seat, because they both wanted to be in the front to paddle, I suddenly slipped. Thankfully I caught myself, however, in catching myself, I dropped the car keys. They landed in the boat, BUT, they then quickly slid around and around until the keys fell through the only hole in the boat. Oh dear! In that bunch of keys was the only key for our car and the only key for our house that I had. I had intended to get more made before this but kept putting it off. Now, they were gone! The children and I prayed for God to help us find our keys. We quickly ran back down the pier and over to the office.

After I related the disastrous problem that had occurred, the man said with a big smile, "You are in luck. We have a diver."

Oh, wow! What a great idea! I hadn't thought of anything like that. "Where is the diver? How can we get him to come?" One question after another flowed from my mouth in my excitement.

The calm and happy man said, "The diver works for several counties. I will put in the request now."

He made a phone call and moments later hung up and told us, "The diver is a woman and she will be here in five hours."

Well, I thought, *five hours is a long time for us, but at least she's coming, so that's good.* The first thing we did was to go out to our Buick and kneel down there in the grass beside it. We prayed that God would help the diver find our keys.

Then Dallas and Katy and I went back down to the pier, climbed back into the paddle boat, and joyfully paddled around the lake. We had a wonderful time, laughing, talking quietly, and watching the ducks, fish, birds, and the beautiful nature all around us. After a while we went back to land. We were quite hungry by now, but decided to try not to think of that since our lunch was neatly packed in the locked car. Again we prayed that God would help find our keys.

While we continued waiting, we had a great time playing on all the playground equipment there: the jungle gym, see-saw, swings, slides, and various other fun things. Dallas especially enjoyed the jungle gym while Katy preferred the swings.

Late in the afternoon, we wandered back over to the office to await the diver. On our way, we said another little prayer. Sure enough, the diver came right on time. She was already dressed in her diving suit, and was very nice and explained to us, "I will do my best to find your keys. But you must understand, there is a six-to-eight-inch layer of silt on the bottom of this lake. Anything as heavy as keys will sink below the silt and cannot be seen. Also, fish are inquisitive little creatures and they always have to check things out.

One could even get the round key chain holder around his nose and swim all the way across the lake with it. So, it's really impossible to find keys or anything that heavy and small in this lake."

I said, "Well, we have been praying."

She flipped her hand and said under her breath, "Well, that won't help." Then she asked where we were when I dropped the keys. We couldn't remember exactly where the paddle boat would have been when we were getting in it and it was drifting around. It was a wide area around the end of the pier. Plus, before I dropped the keys, the boat had drifted out a bit further into the lake. We did our best to give her a place to start.

The diver dipped into the water to get wet, and then dove straight down. There were other people around watching as we waited. Presently, the diver surfaced and threw our keys over onto the pier in front of where we were standing! We were ecstatic! And other people were clapping and shouting.

The diver lifted herself up onto the pier and excitedly shouted to everyone, "YOU'RE NOT GOING TO BELIEVE THIS! YOU'RE NOT GOING TO BELIEVE THIS! THOSE HEAVY KEYS WERE SITTING ON TOP OF THE SILT!"

She looked at me and said, "Prayer DID help!"

My children and I said many "thank-you" prayers that night. We were so very thankful that we had our keys, and we were thankful that we could be a witness to the mighty power of God.

Of course, the first thing we did when we got the car open was to eat our lunch, or rather supper now, and we were super hungry.

"Then they cried unto the LORD in their trouble, and He delivered them out of their distresses" (Ps. 107:6).

First Grade

Ten days after school started, Miss Margaret, Katy's first grade school teacher, called me and said "I need to talk to you about Katy. Can you please come down?"

I responded, "Yes."

"Oh, my," I thought after I hung up the phone. "What could Katy have possibly done?"

My little Katy always did her best to please and do right. She almost never needed a spanking. If she did something wrong, I could look at her and sternly say, "Katy Annette Roberts." That's all I would get out because she would start crying and say, "Oh, Mommy, I'm so sorry!" and whatever it was, she truly tried never to do it again.

So, now what? I prayed as I drove to the school that God would help me handle correctly whatever it was. When I got there, Miss Margaret took me aside and explained.

Evidently, each day when it was time for recess, Miss Margaret would say to the class, "Close your books quietly, and line up at the door. It's time for recess." All the first-graders except Katy would obey. She kept reading and doing her school work. The teacher would always have to repeat the command for Katy, but this time more sternly, "Katy, close your book and line up at the door!" Reluctantly, Katy would obey.

"Until today," Miss Margaret told me. "Today," she continued, "After I spoke to her the second time, Katy stood up beside her desk, put her little hands on her waist, and very firmly but respectfully said to me, 'Miss Margaret, I can play when I get home! I came down here to work.'"

Miss Margaret looked at me and, very puzzled, said, "I have never had a child like that before and I don't know what to say. Most children, all they want to do is play!" Katy dearly loved Miss Margaret and wanted to please and be like her teacher.

I said, "Okay, thank you. I will take care of it." She seemed relieved! So thankful that it wasn't something bad I had to deal with, and actually very proud that my little girl felt that way, I drove home, praying that God would show me how to handle this new situation. I definitely did <u>not</u> want to discourage my daughter from studying, but at the same time she needed to realize how important fresh air and relaxation are to the brain, too. Taking little breaks is also good for the whole body.

When I got home, God impressed me to read from the book, Fundamentals of Education, by Ellen G. White, on page 146, for our family worship time together. Having said nothing to Katy about my discussion with her teacher, that evening I read:

> Youth who are kept in school, and confined to close study, cannot have sound health. Mental effort without corresponding physical exercise, calls an undue proportion of blood to the brain, and thus the circulation is unbalanced. The brain has too much blood, while the extremities have too little. The hours of study and recreation should be carefully regulated, and a portion of the time should be spent in physical labor. When the habits of students in eating and drinking, dressing and sleeping are in accordance with physical law, they can obtain an education without sacrificing health. The

lesson must be often repeated, and pressed home to the conscience, that education will be of little value if there is no physical strength to use it after it is gained.

And, from the book Adventist Home, also by Ellen White, on page 494 we read:

Recreation is essential to best work. The time spent in physical exercise is not lost.… A proportionate exercise of all the organs and faculties of the body is essential to the best work of each. When the brain is constantly taxed while the other organs of the living machinery are inactive, there is a loss of strength, physical and mental. The physical system is robbed of its healthful tone, the mind loses its freshness and vigor, and a morbid excitability is the result.

After I finished reading, I looked up at Dallas sitting in the chair across the room, and then I glanced over at little Katy on the other end of the couch where I was sitting. Katy was GLARING at me.

She paused momentarily, and then said slowly, "Mommy, does Mrs. White REALLY say that?"

I said, "Yes, honey, we just read it in this book."

Very matter of fact and determined, looking out through space like she was telling herself, she said, "Well, okay then, *I will go out for recess.*"

She never knew that I knew anything about her and recess … until maybe this writing…

A few days later, the teacher stopped me at school, took me aside, and said, "What did you do?"

I asked, "Well, what happened?"

She said, "The very next day, when I said, 'children put your books away, it's time for recess,' Katy was the first one to put her books away and the first one in line at the door. It's that way every day now. I never have to tell her twice."

Then Miss Margaret added, "But, Katy's also the first in line to come back in from recess too."

I told Miss Margaret what God had impressed me to read for worship. She, too, was thankful that God had worked it out so beautifully. Both of my children had Miss Margaret for first grade and both dearly loved her. She taught them many good lessons of life, including "Finish what you start before you leave it for good." She helped to train them both to do their very best in life and to totally finish a job.

"Train up a child in the way he should go: and when he is old, he will not depart from it" (Prov. 22:6).

Gift Shop Tragedy

My children and I had the privilege of travelling with their truck-driver daddy many times in their growing-up years. On one such occasion, we had stopped at a truck stop in west Texas out in the "middle of nowhere," about thirty miles from any town. While their daddy fueled up his truck, Dallas, age twelve, and Katy, age seven, and I were checking out the gift shop. Katy was looking at some souvenirs hanging on sharp-pointed prongs.

Someone bumped Katy knocking her into the prong "tree." One prong caught and ripped her nose wide open and a lower prong slit her throat. She screamed and collapsed to the floor in a pool of blood.

I came running from the back of the gift shop. A man had already picked her up and laid her on the counter at the cash register. People had gathered all around her and someone was trying to stop the bleeding.

Right then, her daddy walked in and started asking, "Where is the nearest emergency room?"

The owner of the gift shop said, "It's thirty miles away in the nearest town. I will take you." She kindly asked all the other people to leave and closed the gift shop and drove all four of us in her own car to the hospital.

Katy's daddy sat in front with the driver to find out about the place where we were going. Dallas and I sat in the back seat. I was holding Katy across my lap so I could hold the pressure steady to keep the blood from flowing, and also to keep her calm. I was praying all the way that God would have the right doctors and nurses to work on Katy and that He would guide the doctor's hands to correct this situation as He saw fit.

The staff in the emergency room were very calming, helpful, and efficient. Very soon, the doctor had Katy's nose and throat all sewn up and had given instructions what to do for the swelling and how to take good care of her while it all healed. Soon, we were on our way back to the truck stop and our truck.

Again, God had hand-picked the people to guide and make a blessing out of a tragedy. God used a kind lady willing to *close her shop* and lose customers and money to carry a bleeding little girl in her own car to the emergency room.

"Ye that fear the Lord, trust in the Lord: he is their help and their shield" (Ps. 115:11).

Prayer For A Friend

We had a family friend—I'll call him Will—whose wife had left him. He wanted nothing to do with God, religion, or prayer. Will was the news director for the big radio station in our area. In his mind, he had achieved success on his own—God had done nothing for him, he reasoned—so he wanted nothing to do with the God of heaven. We invited him to church, and even invited him to study the Bible. All was in vain.

BUT Will could *not* stop us from praying for him. He remained our friend, never realizing we still prayed for him. We did this for thirty-two years. Dear reader, if you have a child, husband, wife, mother, father, aunt, uncle, cousin, friend—anyone who does not seem to want God in their life, remember, they cannot stop you from praying for them. Especially,

Remember, they cannot stop you from praying for them.

do *NOT* give up! Time on earth hasn't ended yet and your prayers for him or her are the strongest thing there is.

"The effectual fervent prayer of a righteous man availeth [accomplishes] much" (James 5:16).

Well, one day, after thirty-two years of praying for him, Will called me and sheepishly said, "I don't mean to bother you, but do you think you could ever have time to come over and study the Bible with me?"

BOTHER ME??! HAVE TIME!?! I thought, "Nothing in the world could stop me from studying the Bible with anyone—especially HIM!"

I said, "Yes, of course. I'll be right over!"

Quickly, I grabbed my Bible and a set of printed Bible studies that I kept on hand, and tore off to Will's house, excited and praying all the way. He lived about twenty miles away from us. I had no idea what I was in store for in this new Bible study venture.

After our greetings and some chit-chat, I asked if he had a Bible and would he want to study at the dining room table? He did have a Bible—he had never opened it but "it looked really nice on [his] coffee table." And yes, the dining room table would be fine.

We got seated. Then I prayed and asked God to be with us and help us learn what He wanted us to learn and also to apply what we learned in the way God wanted us to apply it. Then I read the first question. Will didn't even understand the question. After spending twenty minutes trying to explain the question and the answer, Will was yawning and losing interest. He knew nothing of God or the Bible. It all—every word of it—went right over his head.

I tried another type of Bible study. Still no comprehension. Then God hit me with "CHILDREN'S BOOKS!" After all, he IS a babe in Christ. So at home I grabbed the first volume of Arthur Maxwell's *The Bible Story*. You know, those blue books you see in the doctor's offices waiting rooms. They are fantastic! Plus, they have beautiful pictures. My parents bought them for me when I was a child and I still have them. I raised my children on them, too!

That next Bible study at Will's house was a total miracle! His life was changed with the first story in the Bible, the one on Creation. I read the first few chapters on Creation while Will looked at the pictures. After these first chapters, I looked over at Will. He was crying like a baby.

I asked, "Will, what's wrong?"

When he could talk, he asked, "You mean that God made the grass because He loves *ME*?"

I nodded and responded, "Yes."

He asked again, "You mean God made the flowers and trees just for me because He loves *ME*?"

"Yes," I said again.

Never in Will's life had he ever heard that God LOVED HIM. All he had ever been taught about God was vengeance: "You better do this, or God will get you!" and he slapped his fist and hand together in demonstration of vengeance. Or, "You better NOT do that, or God will strike you dead on the spot!" Again, slapping his hands together.

No wonder he didn't want anything to do with God before. Yes, even here in America, where everyone can have a Bible if they want one and can learn about the love of God, is this seventy-eight-year-old man with absolutely no good knowledge of God.

Will and I read and studied more and more each week. He loved it! I did, too, of course. That year, in November, Will was baptized. Through the next eleven months every time I called him (I tried to call every day or two, or visit), I would say, "Whatcha doin?"

He always answered with, "I was just sitting here talking to my Best Friend," or "My Jesus and I were just discussing…"

He was as close to God as I have seen anyone to be. Will told me over and over, "Since I found Jesus, this is the best time of my whole life."

The very next November he died! Will had one whole year with his Jesus.

"They that sow in tears shall reap in joy. He that goeth forth and weepeth, bearing precious seed, shall doubtless come again with rejoicing, bringing his sheaves with him" (Ps. 126:5, 6).

The One Percent

Money was tight! My daddy encouraged me to budget our income, so I worked out a budget. My parents had taught me to give a ten-percent tithe, so I always knew to do that, to give ten percent of my income back to God. Therefore, in this budget, I had ten-percent tithe and then a certain percent for each bill: electric, phone, car, groceries, insurance, and all the others. It always came out exact, with never a penny left over.

Then, while attending some evangelistic meetings, I learned something else about finances. One night the evangelist preached on tithes and offerings. He told us how important it is to give systematic offerings as well as tithe. Well, I thought, "That doesn't mean me because I don't have any money left to give offerings!"

Then I thought, "Well, I better get approval on this way of thinking." So I went to the speaker after the meeting and said, "What you are saying about giving offerings besides the tithe? That doesn't mean me, does it?" and I told him about my lack of money.

He looked at me and said confidently, "Try it!"

Oh, but that is not what I wanted to hear! I wanted him to say, "No, honey, since you don't have enough money, you don't have to do it." But, instead, he said, "Try it."

Oh dear! Now I had better do it, because I wanted to do God's will. The evangelist had said that "God will impress on you how much offering to give. Some will be one, two, or three percent of their income." I prayed that night and asked God how much He wanted me to give for offering. He impressed on me five percent! Wow! Five percent when I didn't think I even had money to do it at all!

Then I sat down and refigured my budget! Ten percent for tithe at the top, and five percent for offering next. Then I adjusted the rest of the bills on down. It came out to six percent left over! Well now, I thought, "I've done something wrong." So I figured again, and again, and lo and behold, it kept coming out to six percent left over!

Finally, after budget figuring for two whole days, it dawned on me that God was giving back to me one percent more than the five percent I was giving Him. For the first time ever I actually had a miscellaneous line in my budget!

You can NOT out-give God! He pours out more blessings than we have room to receive.

"Bring ye all the tithes into the storehouse, that there may be meat in mine house, and prove me now herewith, saith the Lord of hosts, if I will not open you the windows of heaven, and pour you out a blessing, that there shall not be room enough to receive it" (Mal. 3:10).

More blessings!

Well, it gets even better! Figuring ten percent is easy for me—all you have to do is move the decimal. But five percent is a different story. I always call and ask my son, Dallas, "What is five percent of $69.25?" Or "What is five percent of $139.69?" Whatever it was, he would tell me and I would write it down.

One day, after I had asked how much five percent of whatever it was is, Dallas said disgustedly, "Mother, just forget it. Pay ten-percent tithe and ten-percent offering. Then it's the same all the way across the board and you won't have to figure the five percent anymore. I've been giving that for years."

Wow! What a good idea! I've never thought of that before! And my own son is doing it. So, from then on, I have always paid ten-percent tithe and ten-percent offering. And when someone gives me a gift of money, I double tithe because it is a special gift to me. I want to share and give a special gift to God, too!

And like He promises, God pours more blessings on this home and me than I have room to receive! In this way, I have more to share with others.

For example, since the new practice of ten-percent tithe and ten-percent offering, we have always had plenty of food—even when I took food every week to other families that were elderly or handicapped. I was feeding nine people every day. There was always plenty of food. Even if I had not bought it personally, people and angels were bringing it! God always provides. Come, eat with us and see for yourself!

"I have been young, and now am old; yet have I not seen the righteous forsaken, nor His seed begging bread" (Ps. 37:25).

Woolly

Before I had a clothes dryer in the house, I had a six-line clothes line out in the back yard. It was twenty-feet long. There was a vertical metal pole at each end, with a horizontal pole attached. Then came the six lines made out of small cable stretched between the two poles. The lines were about eight inches apart.

One morning, as I was hanging up the first load of clothes which filled the first line and over half of the second line, I noticed a cute woolly worm. He was all pretty and fuzzy, climbing from the ground up the vertical pole. From his determination I could tell he was on a mission of some sort. I affectionately named him Woolly.

When he came to the horizontal pole, he didn't hesitate, but kept up his same pace out to one end of it. He then leaned out over the air from his waist, like he was deciding which of the six lines to take for his trip.

He picked the second one and out he started. He came to the first wooden clothespin, crawled all the way to the top of it and down the other side, then across the smooth, but wet, shirt, up and then over the next clothespin. At the bottom there was a half inch of clothes line, then another tall clothespin, than another shirt, this time with lumps and curves of a still-wet collar, and then another clothespin to go up, over, and down.

He encountered all these high clothes pins and wet clothes, getting all his hundreds of feet sopping wet, over and over as he "moved forward" toward his destination.

About half-way across the line, Woolly ran out of clothes. Whew! From here would be clear sailing, I bet he thought. But immediately, he came to a barrier—Little Red Spider was also on that same clothesline, only going in the opposite direction. They stopped momentarily facing each other, but Woolly had to hurry. He was determined to reach his destination and NO ONE or NOTHING was going to stop him. Woolly simply went under Little Red Spider to the bottom side of the line. After getting around Little Red Spider, Woolly came back up on top of the line and kept going at his same pace.

Little Red Spider sat there for a moment—I guess he was surprised at not having a confrontation with this larger "person."

At last, after all Woolly had gone through, he reached the other side of the clothes line. Bless his little heart! I felt like applauding him. He made it! Yea!!

Watching him made me remember that I, too, am on a journey. I am going to go to heaven. I, too, have turns, curves in the road, rocks, even big boulders to get over. I have hills to climb, and some are even huge mountains. I have deterrents—red and sometimes even black spiders to overcome. Am I as patient, kind, and determined in my journey as Woolly was in his? Or do I get discouraged and give up too quickly? Do I hesitate or second-guess myself about whether I can really do this or not?

Woolly was totally obeying the God that made him. For him we call it instinct. For me it's called the "power of choice." I can choose whether to obey the God that made me. Unlike Woolly, I KNOW my God loves me. Not only did He make me to start with, but then when I rebelled and didn't choose to obey Him, He even died a horrible death for me, to win me back to Him. Now, I have to ask myself, after all my disobedience and wanderings, am I going to come back to Him?

What about you, dear reader? This same God loves you more than anyone else ever could. He died for you, too, to win you back to Him. Will you come home? Will you love Him enough to obey Him? This is how we show Him that we love Him, by obeying Him.

> *This same God loves you more than anyone else ever could. He died for you, too, to win you back to Him.*

"If ye love Me, keep My commandments" (John 14:15).

In Ellen White's book, *Patriarchs and Prophets*, on page 437, we are told:

This experience has a lesson for us. The mighty God of Israel is our God. In Him we may trust, and if we obey His requirements He will work for us in as signal a manner as He did for His ancient people. Everyone who seeks to follow the path of duty will at times be assailed by doubt and unbelief. The way will sometimes be so barred by obstacles, apparently insurmountable, as to dishearten those who will yield to discouragement; but God is saying to such, GO FORWARD. Do your duty at any cost. The difficulties that seem so formidable, that fill your soul with dread, will vanish as you move forward in the path of obedience, humbly trusting in God. (emphasis mine)

Song: LORD I'M COMING HOME by William J. Kirkpatrick

Verse 1:

I've wandered far away from God, Now I'm coming home; The paths of sin too long I've trod, Lord, I'm coming home.

CHORUS:

Coming home, coming home, Nevermore to roam, Open wide Thine arms of love, Lord, I'm coming home.

Verse 2:

I've wasted many precious years, Now I'm coming home; I now repent with bitter tears, Lord, I'm coming home. [Chorus]

Verse 3:

I've tired of sin and straying, Lord, Now I'm coming home; I'll trust Thy love, believe Thy word, Lord, I'm coming home. [Chorus]

Verse 4:

My soul is sick, my heart is sore, Now I'm coming home; My strength renew, my hope restore, Lord, I'm coming home. [Chorus]

God's Caring People

My son was married and my daughter had not yet finished college when suddenly something heartbreaking happened that caused our income to come to a screeching halt. The children's father had left us again, and this time it was permanently.

My daughter and I had no income coming in to pay house bills, buy food, or to pay school bills. Nothing!

Thinking of our bills, the children, and many other things, I realized I didn't know what to do about anything. I threw my hands up toward heaven and through my crying, I said, "God, I don't even know what to do! You just do it!" I didn't know at the time, but that's just exactly what God wants us to do—give everything over to Him to start with and let Him handle it.

People started coming "out of the woodwork" to help! Different people came up to me at church, at school, in town, on the street, and handed me money. And each time it was the exact amount for my next bill. Nobody knew what my bills were. And I thought not many even knew about my dilemma. But God continued to impress people and send them to help me.

One morning, my dear neighbor knocked on the door. When I opened it, she said, after greetings, "What is your largest bill?" I told her, then she said, "Can I see it?" I went and got it and handed it to her. She said, "Thank you, I'll see you later," as she walked toward the door.

I said, "Oh, let me have that bill; I need to pay it."

She said as she left, "No, I'm going to pay it." Bless her heart—that was so super thoughtful of her!

One day, someone gave me forty dollars more than what the next bill was. I was all excited. I thought to myself, "Oh goody, forty dollars! Let's see now, what can I use it for?" I started thinking of things I had been wanting, but "something" told me to keep it. So I did.

My daughter was planning on going to Romania to teach English. Her airline ticket had already been paid for, thankfully, but she still needed certain shots. Two weeks later, she and I went to the Health Department where shots were free. Wouldn't you know, the Health Department had just started charging forty dollars for an office visit? God knew two weeks before that I would need that forty dollars, so He impressed me to keep it! Isn't He awesome?!

Another day, as I was walking down Main Street in town, a man that I knew was walking toward me. We spoke briefly, then suddenly he stopped and said, "Oh, I wanted to help you in some way."

God is always exact and on time!

I replied, "Oh, you don't have to do that." But he was already reaching into his back pocket. He came out with a big wad of paper bills and gently put them in my hand.

I was thanking him profusely when he said, "Oh here, let me see if I have any change." He stuck his hand into his front pocket and brought out a handful of change and put that into my other hand. I thanked him over and over.

When I got back to my car I counted the money he had put in both hands. There was exactly $204.69. The next bill that I needed to pay was exactly $204.69! God is always exact and on time!

There is a saying, "Faith in God includes faith in His timing."

"For thou, LORD, wilt bless the righteous; with favor wilt thou compass him as with a shield" (Ps. 5:12).

Vehicles

With the loss of income mentioned before, also came the loss of my new vehicle. For four months I had nothing to drive except occasionally I could borrow my daughter's Jeep Wrangler. While praying every day for something to drive, I was walking one-and-a-half miles to work. It was good exercise, and it wasn't a problem except when it snowed. Bob, the hospital administrator, found out somehow about my dilemma. He came to me one day and said very sweetly, "I just bought a new van and I would appreciate it if you would drive my old one." WOW! That was a sweet way to put it!

I drove his van for two months, expecting any day for him to come and take it back.

He did come back one day, but instead of taking it, he asked, "Do you like the van?"

I said, "Yes, I love it."

He said, "My wife, Ann, and I have decided to exchange the van for you cleaning our house once a week for thirty months."

I knew that was God using these precious people to help me, because usually people don't make deals like that. Bob and Ann allowed me to drive their van while I was working it off. And they even paid the car insurance during that time. After I worked it off, it was put into my name! It was my very first vehicle I ever owned in my whole life. It was so very exciting! I loved having it and it was a good car. I happily drove it for five more years.

Then one day it got tired and needed some work, so I took it to my mechanic. He checked it out and said, "There are three major things that have gone wrong with it." It would cost thousands of dollars to get it fixed. He told me to go find a good used car and bring it to him and he would check the motor out for me.

That was all just great except that the only thing I know about cars is their color. So, I picked one "kind of pretty" car and took it to the mechanic. He informed me that "it's getting ready to kick the bucket, too."

I started praying, "Dear Lord, please help me find the right car." One night I was putting one of my patients to bed, when on her TV the advertiser was saying, "You can buy a brand-new Kia for $111.00 a month." *Wow*, I thought, *I can afford that.*

So, the next morning, I grabbed my daddy and a friend and ran to the nearest Kia sales lot in Asheville, North Carolina. I ran in the door all excited. A man came toward me and said, "May I help you?"

Enthusiastically, I blurted out, "I want the one that's $111.00 a month."

The man rolled his eyes; he looked at me and said, "Lady, that's the Kia in Greer."

"Well, if they can do it there, you can do it, too," I thought.

Then he said, "To get that kind of a deal, you have to put $5,000 down." Oh my, I had never even seen $5,000. Then he said, "And besides that, you have to trade in another Kia."

Well, the advertisement had not said any of that, that I saw, anyway.

My countenance fell through the floor. I was about to cry and turned to leave, when he said, "Well, come here, let me show you what we have."

"Well, I can't afford a new car," I said as I fought back the tears.

He said, "Come here." He took me outside to the car lot and showed me the cheapest one they had. It didn't have power steering nor air conditioning. But I didn't care. I needed something to drive to work.

So the salesman and I got in and took off around the block. I struggled with the "manual" steering. But it was okay. I thought, "I can just work up muscles in my arms and I'll be fine with this car."

When we got back to the car lot, the salesman, who had noticed my steering struggles, looked at me and said, "Lady, you can't drive this! Let me show you another one." He took me to a white Kia Spectra with air conditioning and power steering—the only one on the lot with a REBATE. He let me use the REBATE for a down payment. Inside the office, another man set up monthly payments for me. When he told me what they were it was more money than I even made in a month.

I said tearfully, "I can't afford that" and started to leave again.

But the man said, "Wait, sit down; we will work something else out."

They let me trade in the van that Bob and Ann helped me get. The dealership ended up lowering the payments three times, down to something I could afford. God got me a brand-new vehicle that only had fifteen miles on it! I had a new car thanks to God's mercy and putting the right people, including Bob and Ann, in the right places at the right times. God is so awesome!

"Therefore I say unto you, what things soever ye desire, when ye pray, believe that ye receive them, and ye shall have them" (Mark 11:24).

God Provided Jobs

God also provided jobs for me during the time of financial crisis referred to in the other story. One day, the Director of Home Health called and said she was looking for someone to do medical records in their office. Would I be interested?

I prayed about it, and realizing that God was handing me a job, I called back and accepted. It was an amazing job. All the other office people were so kind and helpful. God helped me learn quickly. It was a part-time job in the mornings.

A few days later, God also worked out that a lady asked if I would stay with her mother and help her to do a few things. That, too, was a great job and part time.

Then, one after another, different retired people were asking for help for various things: help driving them to the store or to a doctor's appointment, help bathing, help writing letters, help cooking. it was just all sorts of fun things. I enjoyed every one of them.

After two-and-a-half years in the medical records field, the hospital changed systems and two of us lost our jobs. Even so, I was thankful that God had worked that job out for me at that point in my life. It got my mind back into the business world. After raising my children all those years, going into precise and exacting work was very good for me. I had to double check doctors', nurses', and therapists' signatures and dates and remind them of changes, among many other things. God knew that I needed that.

When that job ended I was already established with five retired people, helping them in their own homes. Then soon a sixth one asked for help. I thoroughly enjoyed helping people, and these part time jobs built up more and more hours through the years until I was literally working 107–110 hours a week. It was paying all my bills and I loved the work.

However, I was getting more and more tired. One night I dropped to my knees exhausted, and prayed, "Dear God, if there is any way I can slow down and still pay the bills, please work something out."

Two mornings later, a ninety-one-year-old lady called from another town an hour away and asked, "I understand you cook vegan?"

I said, "Yes."

She responded, "And you have 3ABN* on your television?"

I said, "Yes."

She said, "Can I move in with you and you stay home and just take care of me?"

WOW! I had never thought of that before. I love to cook and never got to be home long enough to cook. I always carried nuts, raisins, bananas, and apples in my car to eat as I drove to the next client's house. So I prayed and God impressed me to let that lady move in with me!

"But they that wait upon the Lord shall renew their strength; they shall mount up with wings as eagles; they shall run, and not be weary; and they shall walk, and not faint" (Isa. 40:31).

I gave my two-weeks' notice to my six clients. One of them decided to come and stay with me, also. My son and daughter had grown up and left home and my husband was gone, so there I was in a four-bedroom house all alone—but not for long! God immediately started filling up the bedrooms. Plus, He increased my income to four times as much!

I got two rooms ready and M and L (I will call them Millie and Lucy) both moved into my house. I had planned ahead a schedule of breakfast at 8:00 a.m., dinner at 1:00 p.m., and supper at 6:00 p.m. I thought they should keep the same schedule they had had at their previous homes. However, Millie and Lucy, at ninety-one and ninety years old, didn't even wake up until 10:30 in the morning. So, I decided we would make a schedule to fit them. After all, this is now their home and they should feel like it is so that they could be relaxed and enjoy their lives.

We had such a good time! For the first six weeks we had no repeat meals. When they felt like it they would help in the kitchen, and we would make all kinds of healthy dishes. God provided people to come play the piano for us on some days. We had a good time singing and praising God.

Through all those years, God kept His little family-care home full. When one room was empty, God immediately sent someone else to fill that room. One time, on the day after one of the bedrooms became vacant, I received a call from a lady in Missouri asking, "Do you have an empty room?"

I said, "Yes."

She said, "I want to reserve it for this next weekend."

Confused, I asked, "For your mother or father?" She answered, "For my husband and me." Confused even more, I said "You want me to take care of you and your husband?"

Now *she* was confused and said, "No, we just want a room for the weekend."

I replied, "Who do you think you called?" She said the name of our local motel. It turns out that the motel's phone number is only one number different than mine. I said, "Oh, I'm sorry, this is a family-care home."

She and I had a big laugh, I told her the correct number for the motel, and she laughingly said, "I can't believe I almost put my husband and myself in a family-care home.!"

I never advertised. I never had to. God always provided the clients. Then, for an added blessing, my daddy came to live with me, so not only did God provide enjoyable and loving work for me, He also worked it out so I could make an income while I also took care of my precious daddy!

God is SO AWESOME!

"Blessed is the man that walketh not in the counsel of the ungodly, nor standeth in the way of sinners, nor sitteth in the seat of the scornful. But his delight is in the law of the LORD; and in His law doth he meditate day and night. And he shall be like a tree planted by the rivers of water, that bringeth forth his fruit in his season; his leaf also shall not wither; and whatsoever he doeth shall prosper" (Ps. 1:1–3).

*Three Angels Broadcasting Network.

Lightning

Lightning is beautiful. I love watching it, but not feeling it!

At this writing, I have been struck by lightning four times—one time while I was driving my car, and the other three times I was talking on the telephone.

On a bright, sunny day, with no clouds in the sky, I was driving to the post office. As I was slowly crossing the railroad tracks, a bolt of beautiful lightning flashed across the sky and struck through the windshield and hit my left hand, burning my thumb. The pain was sharp and it hurt for a while. But I realized that God again was with me. My left hand was on the steering wheel at the level of my heart, which the lightning bolt could have hit. Plus, only my thumb was burned and not my whole hand.

Thanksgiving Day comes many times a year in my life, not just in November.

I mentioned that I have been struck by lightning three times while talking on the phone. The first two times I was struck by lightning while on the phone, the bolt came through the line, hurting my ear and giving me a bad headache. Eventually the pain went away, but now, when I hear thunder and see lightning, I try to get off the phone as soon as possible.

Thanksgiving Day comes many times a year in my life, not just in November.

The last time a bolt of lightning hit my phone, I was just telling the other person "There's a storm. We must hang up," when BANG, the lightning hit my phone and me! The pain in my head was severe. The phone went dead and my hearing was totally gone!

I lay down on the floor to keep from fainting with the pain. After what seemed like hours, the pain in my head subsided, but I still had no hearing in the right ear. I prayed that God would restore my hearing. During the next twenty-four hours, little by little, my hearing returned.

Then the next day a telephone repairman came out to fix the phone in response to my call. He was out on my back porch working when he called me and said, "Lady, look at this!" I walked over to him and looked where he was pointing on the side of my house. There, where the telephone wires and controls used to be in the box, was only black ashes!

The man looked at me and said, "It's a good thing you were not on the phone when this happened. If anyone had been on the phone, this would have killed them instantly!" I told him that I WAS on the phone. He said, "Wow, you sure are lucky!"

I said, "I don't believe in luck. It had to be God in my life."

"You are right about that!" he exclaimed.

God is so awesome! He had saved my life again.

"Therefore will I give thanks unto Thee, O Lord, among the heathen, and sing praises unto thy name" (Ps. 18:49).

Jeep Slide

Early one brisk, cold morning, I borrowed my daughter's Jeep Wrangler to drive up our mountain to feed the pets of some friends who were out of town. This morning was different in that the road my friends lived on had just been newly paved with a few inches of loose gravel on top.

I shifted the gears down at the steepest part of the mountain to continue climbing. The Jeep stalled and started sliding backwards out of the curve. As it picked up speed sliding down the road in the loose gravel, I tried everything I could think of to stop—but nothing worked. I prayed, "God help me. Please don't let me wreck my daughter's Jeep." Momentarily, the Jeep slid off the road and turned up on the passenger side. It had slid about 200 feet. I was relieved when I saw a small tree that the Jeep had turned over onto. I was hoping the tree was strong enough to hold the jeep from flipping over and going down the side of the mountain. The two driver's side wheels were three to four feet up in the air with the driver side up, so I had to very carefully and slowly climb up and out of the Jeep.

When my feet were safely on the ground and the Jeep had not rolled on down the mountain from all my pushing and pulling trying to get out, I walked around to see the damage to the Jeep from the tree stopping the fall. To my shocked amazement, the tree had not stopped (held) the Jeep from tumbling on down the mountainside. And, by the way, I saw about twenty feet down that mountain was a huge metal culvert sticking out of the side of the mountain, straight below where the Jeep and I were. If the tree had not stopped us, we would have hit that and maybe even broken the Jeep in two! But wait! I was just saying that the tree had not stopped us. I discovered, walking around the turned over Jeep, that the Jeep was two feet from that tree, and was still literally balancing on the two wheels of the passenger side!

Even after all my tugging and pulling to get myself out, the Jeep kept its balance on two wheels on the brink of a mountainside drop-off! What stopped it? What kept it still while I pulled and pushed and wiggled around to get out? You and I both know! It was God's angels protecting not only me, but also the Jeep from a very bad accident.

I called my son and he came, and God helped him pull the Jeep back over onto all four wheels with his truck and then pull it up and out of the downward slope, with no dents or damage at all to the Jeep!

"The angel of the LORD encampeth round about them that fear him, and delivereth them" (Ps. 34:7).

The Napkin Wadder

"Excuse me, Sir. Could I have another napkin?" I asked the waiter. What a luxury to simply be able to ask for a napkin! But at home I have to get up from the table and get my own napkin. Up. Down. Up. Down! I get up to go to the kitchen to get more bread, sitting down again. Then get up to bring more hot, mashed potatoes. Then back down!

Every time someone needs something, I'm immediately up, grabbing my napkin from my lap and wadding it a little as I lay it on the table. Then I sit back down and try to straighten out my napkin enough to lay it on my lap again. Or sometimes I just hold it wadded in my lap as I eat with the other hand. Then I get up, nervously trying to remember again what I forgot to put on the table.

Then up to answer the phone. Down. Up to answer the doorbell. Back down. Up. Down. Up. Down, through the whole meal. My poor napkin is riddled, the next one is riddled, and the next; I've been known to use six or seven paper napkins at one meal, wadding them from nervousness.

One day, I read in *Desire of Ages* where "…God's purposes know no haste and no delay" (White, p. 32). That means, too, that Jesus, sent from God, also knew no haste and no delay. Now how did He do that? I want to be like Him. Jesus was calm, patient, kind, and loving. There is no record of Him wadding napkins in frustration. Well, God took me all the way to the United Kingdom to teach me to calm down. Of course, He could have taught it to me here at home in North Carolina, but I was too busy and didn't have time to learn.

My daughter and I took a vacation to the United Kingdom as her present for finishing graduate school. Over there I was dependent on trains and buses to get around and had to sit and wait as long as five hours at a time. So, what could a "napkin wadder" do during that time? Well, of course the first few times I had to wait, I "stewed" for a while, then expressed my impatience verbally to whoever was around me, Then I would talk about something unrelated, like the weather. Then glance at my watch. To my jittery self it had only been half an hour, we still had four-and-a-half hours to wait. Then I came up with a more productive use of my time. I started helping my daughter study for her national board exam for physical therapy that she would take when we would return to the states. I would ask her questions from the notes she had brought along for times like these. Pretty soon we were laughing and enjoying the whole situation.

After experiencing several similar situations, it started dawning on my stubborn self that I could leave off the first two reactions, the "stewing" and verbalization. Negative statements never uplift or help anyone. And the mental "stewing" did me no good, either, except to give me a headache and raise my blood pressure.

So, after a few days of this, I finally "got the hang of" what God was patiently trying to teach me. When I have to wait for the train or anything—no wait, lets rephrase that—when I need to wait—I can smile, laugh, say "oops," and stay pleasant, realizing that's part of my education in learning to be heaven bound—becoming more like Jesus.

This new attitude God has given me will keep my blood pressure down and encourage the person or people around me, rather than adding to their stress and misery, not to mention my own!

And guess what? I've also noticed at the dinner table that I no longer wad my napkin. Yea! Now my napkin usage is no longer as expensive as my meal.

"And the peace of God, which passeth all understanding, shall keep your hearts and minds through Christ Jesus" (Phil. 4:7).

Epilogue

God hasn't stopped being in my life just because this book ended. He is still here. Maybe there will be a second volume. But while you wait, think about how God is in YOUR life and write your own book. God is with you! Just take a moment to look around!

"...Blessing, and glory, and wisdom, and thanksgiving, and honour, and power, and might, be unto our God for ever and ever. Amen" (Rev. 7:12).

TEACH Services, Inc.
P U B L I S H I N G

We invite you to view the complete
selection of titles we publish at:
www.TEACHServices.com

We encourage you to write us
with your thoughts about this,
or any other book we publish at:
info@TEACHServices.com

TEACH Services' titles may be purchased in
bulk quantities for educational, fund-raising,
business, or promotional use.
bulksales@TEACHServices.com

Finally, if you are interested in seeing
your own book in print, please contact us at:
publishing@TEACHServices.com

We are happy to review your manuscript at no charge.

CPSIA information can be obtained
at www.ICGtesting.com
Printed in the USA
BVHW062354170619

551270BV00006B/28/P

9 781479 609727